Letters to Children in Family Therapy

of related interest

How and Why Children Fail
Edited by Ved Varma
ISBN 1 85302 108 3 hb
ISBN 1 85302 186 5 pb

How and Why Children Hate
Edited by Ved Varma
ISBN 1 85302 116 4 hb
ISBN 1 85302 185 7 pb

Children, Bereavement and Trauma
Nurturing Resilence
Paul Barnard, Ian Marland and Julie Nagy
ISBN 1 85302 785 5

Using Interactive Imagework with Children
Walking on the Magic Mountain
Deborah Plummer
ISBN 1 85302 671 9

Helping Children to Build Self-Esteem
A Photocopiable Activities Book
Deborah Plummer
ISBN 1 85302 927 0

Understanding and Supporting Children with Emotional and Behavioural Difficulties
Edited by Paul Cooper
ISBN 1 85302 666 2 pb
ISBN 1 85302 665 4 hb

Group Work with Children and Adolescents
A Handbook
Edited by Kedar Nath Dwivedi
Foreword by Robin Skynner
ISBN 1 85302 157 1

Active Analytic Group Therapy for Adolescents
John Evans
Foreword by Peter Wilson
ISBN 1 85302 616 6 pb
ISBN 1 85302 615 8 hb

Letters to Children in Family Therapy

A Narrative Approach

Torben Marner

Jessica Kingsley Publishers
London and Philadelphia

The right of Torben Marner to be identified as author of this work has been asserted by him in accordance with the Copyright, Designs and Patents Act 1988.

First published in the United Kingdom in 2000 by
Jessica Kingsley Publishers Ltd,
116 Pentonville Road, London
N1 9JB, England
and
325 Chestnut Street,
Philadelphia PA 19106, USA.

www.jkp.com

Library of Congress Cataloging in Publication Data
A CIP catalog record for this book is available from the Library of Congress

British Library Cataloguing in Publication Data
A CIP catalogue record for this book is available from the British Library

ISBN 1 85302 894 0

Printed and Bound in Great Britain by
Athenaeum Press, Gateshead, Tyne and Wear

Contents

Dedication

To my father and mother for the happiness and sorrow of my childhood; to Lotte, Joakim, Kristoffer and the coming grandchild for the warmth and meaning to my life; and to all the children and parents who have let me use their stories and letters to help other children and families around the world.

My thanks to Natasha whose picture of 'The Uninvited Guest' decorates the chapter titles of this book.

Preface

In recent years I have enjoyed teaching a technique known as the narrative approach to family therapy in Denmark, Norway, England and the Czech Republic. I have frequently conducted a one-day workshop in which I have talked about the theory and practice of Michael White and David Epston (who pioneered this technique) in the morning and have instructed the participants in couples or small groups to create a therapeutic letter in the afternoon. Using a little support to encourage participants to make good letters into impressive ones has been the best positive feedback to my teaching that I could ever get. In response to questions from my good friend Susan George (an American psychologist and child psychotherapist) about my letter-writing to children in family therapy I began e-mail a series of letters that became more and more of a manual of why and how I write post-sessional therapeutic letters.

That e-mailed account grew into this book. It was never meant to be an academic study with precise sources of reference and a comprehensive overview of the present field of family therapies. The idea has been to give an introduction to narrative therapy and a sort of manual for letter-writing to children in family therapy. For this purpose each chapter has a vignette-like theoretical reflection or description of an aspect of the practice of narrative therapy and a series of instructive letters.

The book is written for young therapists who are searching for a foothold in the fascinating but interminable landscape of therapies, as well as for experienced therapists checking out the narrative approach in order to see if there should be something that could serve as an inspiration and a supplement to their personal ideology and style of working.

Introduction

Dear Susan,

On the last day of our meeting in Copenhagen you mentioned that a six-year-old girl, Cynthia, whom you have in play therapy, recently told you that she has the most awful nightmares. That took me back to Reykjavik in Iceland 1993 and another six-year-old girl whom I helped to rid of her nightmares with a single supportive letter. Here is a copy of the letter which I promised to send to you:

> Dear Helga,
>
> You are so young that you do not yet understand Danish, so I will let your mother read my letter to you.
>
> It was amusing to meet you and playact for you. You are a nice and clever girl who manages many things, but your mother has mentioned to me that you occasionally allow Nightmares to outwit you during the night. Luckily, Nightmares are a little stupid and therefore it is possible for children to learn how to cheat them!
>
> Nightmares are so foolish that they believe that they only bring exciting and interesting dreams, and so stupid they are that they believe that they have the right to rule over you.
>
> But I will tell you what you can do when they try to rule over you and give you dreams which YOU don't like but THEY think are really funny and exciting. You can call on your mother and father or go to their bedroom like you

used to do…but it would be even better to get hold of a little cardboard box with a key hole! You see, Nightmares are not only stupid, they are also very curious – so if you say to them, when they come to rule over you: 'Behold my box!' they are SO curious that they slip through the keyhole and SO stupid that they cannot find their way out again! And then you and your mother and father can drive into the countryside once in a while and set them free there!

In that way you will be the one who is in charge and when you have become a good Nightmare-catcher you can maybe help some friends of yours who also for a period of time have let themselves be outwitted by these foolish Nightmares who love to rule over children.

Good luck with catching Nightmares!

Your friend

Torben

Eight months later I received a letter from Helga's mother. She ended her letter by writing: 'Your idea to help my little Helga has had fantastic results – she has not had any wicked dreams since I read your letter to her!! She still has her dreambox on her bedside table and I have overheard her telling a friend who had the same problem how she got rid of her nightmares, and she added "…and it is important that it is your parents who help you". I am looking forward to seeing you again.'

Since then I have used variations of this letter in Denmark, England and the Czech Republic to help children become stronger than their persecuting nightmares.

And, by the way, when I revisited Iceland two years later Helga was still free of her nightmares and was proud to show me her cardboard box.

Torben

PART 1

My Point of Departure

The Works of Michael White and David Epston

Theories of Narrative Therapy

CHAPTER I

Source of Inspiration
Gregory Bateson

Dear Torben,

It is your generous use of your imagination that surprises me most in your letter. You so directly set up the nightmares in the child's mind as discrete and easy-to-hate enemies. And your directions to Helga were so clear for her to follow. I imagine she could picture in her head the nightmare-catching box as her mother read her your letter. Please tell me the process you go through when you create letters like these. How do the ideas and images come to you? And are there certain basic principles you follow?

Susan

Dear Susan,

In a few lines you have put questions to me in a way that has inspired me to explore the process of letter-writing and I intend to send you a few theoretical reflections which have influenced me as well as a series of letters which, I hope, in the end will provide you with a useful answer to your questions.

For some time after I returned to Denmark from Reykjavik in 1993, having created the idea of a box to catch nightmares in, I felt very creative. But suddenly I remembered a sequence of a video shown in Elsinore in 1989 during the first workshop which the Australian family therapist Michael White gave in Denmark. On this video I had seen Michael White ask a six-year-old boy who sat with a black box in his hand permission to hold it. I watched Michael White taking the box in which a Temper Tantrum had been caught – he had so much difficulty holding the box that he fell down from his chair! Quickly he handed back the box to the child who stared sceptically at him while shaking his head.

Luckily my unconscious memory hadn't forgotten that scene – and ever since I have allied myself with young children and adolescents towards their persecuting Trolls, Monsters and other personalized problems and have proposed various forms of boxes to catch them in, hence leaving the children to decide their own destiny. Later on I have come to think upon that many ethnic cultures from the dawn of days have had their means to catch evil dreams, as for example the native Americans who have their net of feathers.

Like Michael White and his colleague, friend and co-author David Epston from New Zealand, my career as a family therapist has followed the history of family therapy. In the late 1960s I was influenced by the strategic ideas by Jay Haley (Haley 1963); in the 1970s the structural family therapy by Salvador Minuchin (Minuchin 1978) made an impact on my work; and in the 1980s I was influenced by the systemic ideas of The Milan Associates (Palazzoli *et al.* 1980).

But alongside that, an essential part of my training as a child psychiatrist in the early 1970s was play therapy and individual child therapy. Maybe this is why I so easily grasped the theory and practice of narrative therapy as described in the books of Michael White and David Epston. Through this form of therapy I obtained direct contact with the child but in the presence of the parents and siblings.

In their first book, *Narrative Means to Therapeutic Ends* (White and Epston 1990), Michael White and David Epston have given a short but rich description of their sources of inspiration. In this letter I will tell you a few things about the influence of some of the ideas of the anthropologist Gregory Bateson.

Gregory Bateson and the cybernetic theorists described a snowball effect: a process in which a deviation is increased due to a mutual feedback and ends up being a problem. Any search for the cause of the problem becomes part of the aetiology of the problem, because it leads to vicious circles of guilt, shame and feelings of failure.

Besides the externalization of the problem, Michael White and David Epston emphasized from early on the importance of the 'unique outcomes'. These are moments where the child defies the tyrannical claims of the problem. The unique outcomes were explained in the light of the notion of 'cognitive maps'. These maps act as a frame of interpretation which determines the meaning given to different experiences and events. If experiences do not fit well-known patterns they do not become facts for us. This is why the unique outcomes are not valued and do not become facts for us until they are highlighted in the family sessions. And here they serve as proofs for a power balance in favour of the child and not the problem.

Even though, in all their books, Michael White and David Epston describe the essential usefulness of the written text in the therapeutic process, and provide a lot of examples, it took me some years before I began to use postsessional or therapeutic letters on a regular basis. At first I worked primarily on improving my externalizing dialogues and creative ideas to contribute to the free-dom-fight of the child. Let me give you an example from 1993.

Case History: Nikolaj

The parents brought their child, 11-year-old Nikolaj, to therapy because he was suffering from obsessional rituals, school phobia and stuttering. Both parents had been married before. The mother's adolescent son lived with his father and Nikolaj's father had an adolescent daughter who lived with his ex-wife and her new husband. Nikolaj's father had had the painful experience in his first marriage of losing his first son by sudden death at four months old. Therefore Nikolaj was a 'precious baby' and his father was rather over-protective – which he discussed openly in the first of seven family therapy sessions.

In the first session the notion of the 'Troll' was intro-duced. The Troll made Nikolaj perform his obsessional rituals and was sabotaging his going to school. The rituals consisted of meticulous wanderings up and down the indoor stairs of the house. The Troll as a phenomenon was at once accepted by Nikolaj and his parents. Nikolaj described how the power of the Troll was expanding and now demanded that both parents should stay with him at home. I declared that I experienced all three of them as a closely attached, loving family which for a period of time was feeling stressed by being enlarged by yet another family member, the Troll, and that would be too much for any small family.

A metaphor of a campaign with many battlefields was developed, and I suggested that Nikolaj and his allies, the parents, should fight in one place at a time. They chose the school attendance and Nikolaj and his mother decided to contact a schoolfriend and make him an extra ally. In the second family session it was still the Troll who had the upper hand. The father expressed an irritation towards its power in their home and a wonder that the Troll apparently had no power when Nikolaj was visiting his grandparents. The Troll had made Nikolaj torment his father, insisting that he should not join a five-day seminar. The father said that Nikolaj had given him a bad conscience by telling him that if he went to the seminar he would work on the side of the Troll!

The mother stated that neither the Troll nor Nikolaj could make her feel guilty. The family was invited to pretend that they were quite an ordinary family until the following family session. In the third session all the three of them talked smilingly about the home task as a mutually accepted defeat. Then the father said that the last days had been very positive and Nikolaj explained that his rituals were reduced in number and that he now slept in his own bed the whole night.

With regard to the school attendance Nikolaj had begun to go to school by himself. At the end of the conversation the father asked some advice: whether he should phone the parents of Nikolaj's schoolmates in order to arrange that they would come visiting him. (This was a year before I read the article by David Epston 'Temper tantrum: Saving face, losing face and going off your face' (Epston and White

1992). In this article David Epson proposes inviting schoolmates to a party to see a fit of the child's rituals. In order to avoid this the child would rather fight against his symptoms and hereby regain his freedom and self-control.) On this occasion I only emphasized the importance of expanding Nikolaj's area of actions as he had started to play with friends outside the home. Some weeks later in the fourth session the parents informed me that the rituals were reduced to almost nothing and that the Troll, whom the parents now talked about almost as a family member, had lost a lot of its restraining influence. What was left was only that now and then, when Nikolaj was asked to take his plate from the table to the kitchen might he insist that it was not possible for him. In doing this he showed that he was able to get the Troll as his ally! Nikolaj laughed when I gave this description. His school attendance was now quite normal.

Seven weeks later the family came to the fifth session. Nikolaj looked relaxed and happy and had grown in many ways. Everything functioned outside the home. Inside the home the Troll still had a grip on Nikolaj, now and then forcing him to repeat sequences of actions the other way round. Nikolaj said that he was really fed up with this. Contrary to the parents' opinion he didn't think that his parents were able to observe when it was him and not the Troll who was in command. This led to a prediction task in which we decided that the family members should keep a secret diary with a plus sign (+) when they thought that Nikolaj would be in command and a minus sign (–) if they thought it would be the Troll who was ruling, in order to see who would make the best prediction.

As Nikolaj talked a lot about his rituals every day, the parents agreed to a talking time of ten minutes a day during which they would listen to Nikolaj without any comments.

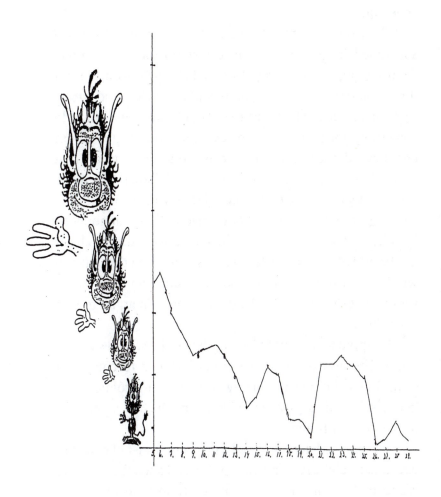

Figure 1.1 Registration scheme showing the decline in power of the Troll

Finally it was agreed that Nikolaj and his father would make a graph of the relationship between the strength of Nikolaj and the Troll.

Four weeks later they came for the sixth session. Nikolaj brought an impressive graph on which all of them had made their predictions. These were used to indicate that there had been days where the influence of Nikolaj had been sovereign.

When the parents told me that one day the Troll had succeeded in getting Nikolaj to restrain the two of them from jogging in the forest I backed the parents up in not 'breaking down' but being more and more clear and strong in their attitude. Moreover they should now and then do something for themselves: for example, they might go out and have dinner together. The parents didn't think that Nikolaj could be left on his own, but Nikolaj solved the problem by declaring that he could stay with an aunt for the evening. In the seventh and last session Nikolaj announced happily that all that was left of the Troll were the two hairs on the end of its tail; and the parents confirmed that Nikolaj was in good spirits, that he had done some domestic work spontaneously and showed a great interest in arguing with his father.

The approaching trial of strength was the school summer camp. The previous year the father had had to come and bring Nikolaj home after a day and a half. I recommended 'rehearsals' and suggested to Nikolaj that he take a photo of his parents with him.

Four months later I received a postcard from Nikolaj who wrote with childish misspellings: 'Dear Toben, I am on the island of Ore and have seen the bottleship museum. The Troll has gone and I am only slightly homsick. Greetings, Nikolaj.'

This case history from 1993 has components from my structural and my systemic work as well as from my early readings of the books by Michael White and David Epston.

After 1993 I began as often as possible to supplement my family sessions with a therapeutic letter to the child or the adolescent.

Torben

CHAPTER 2

Source of Inspiration
Michel Foucault

Dear Susan,

In *Narrative Means to Therapeutic Ends* Michael White and David Epston have described how reading the works of the French writer and philosopher Michel Foucault has influenced their theory and practice. Michel Foucault has provided them with the following statement: knowledge = power = suppression. In accordance with this they have emphasized that, by being invisible, the modern practice of power, which is found everywhere in society, is able to form 'truths' which become accepted in our culture and shape our lives and relationships. This is why the problem-filled story becomes powerful by its 'objective value of truth', demands all our attention and thereby is suppressing. And people often accept this suppression because it is experienced not as a result of power, but more as a feeling of fulfilment and liberation as, for example, reported by sufferers of anorexia nervosa.

This power, however, can be deconstructed by the use of externalizing dialogues which move the objectification and 'thingification' from the person to the problem. Michel Foucault himself was not interested in the changing lives of people but nonetheless his ideas have inspired Michael

White and David Epston to view the problem as an enemy and suppressor and to join forces with the child and the family against the problem.

Michael White has stated that 'the problem is the problem' because it creates new problems. An example of this could be an anxiety in a child that may lead to isolation, over-protection and attempts by the parents to spare the child from anxiety-provoking situations, which again may lead to feelings of failure in the child. The parents may feel guilty in their belief that they have done something wrong and thus the anxiety becomes a problem which creates more problems.

Instead of considering the function of anxiety, Michael White has focused on the fact that in order for the problem to survive it needs somebody to react to it. If you do react, you become a support and an ally to the problem. As long as the problem is in command it will survive. If you refuse to cooperate, the context changes and the power of the problem is undermined.

The therapist may help to reduce the implications of knowledge = power = suppression by deconstructing the expert knowledge. The therapist may achieve this by positioning himself as a 'co-author' and by facilitating a context in which the child becomes the privileged author of his or her alternative and preferred story.

Case History: Ole

Ole was an 11-year-old boy who was referred to me for temper tantrum, school refusal and soiling.

In the first session Ole turned out to be an intelligent and initially somewhat sceptical child. Swiftly, however, he grasped my idea of isolating three of his enemies: Fear, Shyness and Temper Tantrum Monster. The latter got its name because I acknowledged a natural age-appropriate quest for autonomy.

These three enemies had succeeded, I learnt from him, in ensuring that he did not attend school, that he had no friends and moreover that his toilet habits had been so poorly developed that he could not join the other boys in the swimming pool, use short trousers, etc.

When Ole asked me whether he would have to go on fighting and winning battles for the rest of his life, I explained to him that the many children to whom I had been an ally had told me that it is mostly in the beginning that you have to be on guard and fight each time the enemies sneak up to you and make you do things you really do not want to do. Then the enemies will crumple, turn pale, their knees shake with fear and they will be easy to beat.

At the end of the session I gave Ole a letter which contained the names of his three enemies: Fear, Shyness and Temper Tantrum Monster and instructions of two things he could do to beat the Temper Tantrum Monster:

- When he felt a temper tantrum approaching in the company of his mother in the drawing room he could outwit the Temper Tantrum Monster by going back to his own room where he would be in command with a natural autonomy.

- When he felt that he was about to soil his trousers he should pretend he was going to the kitchen but on his way he should slip into the restroom, shut the door behind him and use the toilet.

During the conversation I had described how the door to my office has a bewitched threshold so that neither Fear, Shyness nor Temper Tantrum Monster could enter and therefore Ole could speak with his natural voice. This was repeated several times during the conversation and to emphasize it I walked out of the office in front of him and his mother and blocked the way to the corridor so that they could slip through the door to the stairs before the Monster could catch them.

In the second session with Ole a month later I asked casually: 'Ole, what day in August is the start of your school?' Ole answered: 'In a week and I am looking forward to it'. Now Ole told me with pride that he had not been soiling the last nine days but had used the toilet in the proper way.

Ole asked me whether I thought that the Temper Tantrum Monster was able to learn the tricks he was using in this period of time to slip into the restroom. I told him that the monsters who had taken command over him were like Norwegian Trolls, difficult to move but also stupid. And that, just like colour photos from the 1950s, they would grow paler and eventually fade away. Over the course of the next three conversations the school attendance was normalized and a few months later a follow-up session showed that everything was all right. The mother was pleased that the Temper Tantrum Monster had gone and Ole gave me a parcel containing Christmas cakes he had baked himself.

Writing this, I remember that I got the idea of the bewitched threshold from David Epston a few years earlier during a workshop in which I was amused and inspired by his playful conversations with children and youngsters.

Later the same year of 1993, when I had started to write postsessional therapeutic letters to the children referred to me, I had a funny experience.

Case History: Henrik

The mother of nine-year-old Henrik was admitted for the first time for a manic-depressive psychosis, and Henrik was in fostercare during her hospitalization. He was referred to me for soiling and I invited him, his mother, her contact nurse and the fostermother to one of four sessions.

Dear Henrik,

It was great fun and exciting to talk with you. It's a long time since I have talked to a smart boy like you who is not yet ten years old and already knows how to cheat Trolls and Monsters!

Before I got a chance to tell you, you told me that you can just pretend to head for the kitchen and then jump into the restroom and slam the door behind you before the Troll becomes aware!

Since you also are good at running we agreed that you should compete against the Troll at running (he is big and heavy and therefore easy to outrun) when you are in the playground and feel like going to the restroom.

I have great expectations that you will regain your strength and win the fight and that the Troll will shrink, turn pale and shiver more and more each time you cheat it.

I am looking forward to our next meeting.

Your ally

Torben

Reading my postsessional letter to Henrik, Susan, you too must be surprised by his ingenuity!

Torben

CHAPTER 3

Source of Inspiration
Narratology

Dear Susan,

In this chapter I will outline a third source of inspiration which has had maybe the greatest influence on the theory and practice of Michael White and David Epston. It stems from the concept of narratology. Increasingly over the last century the notion of narration and narrative has become a central metaphor in all fields of human thinking – as in the grand tales of literature, in the psychic myths of Freud and Jung, in philosophy (e.g. in the works of Paul Ricoeur) and in the practice of field work in anthropology, to indicate the width of the range.

Michael White and David Epston began to use the concept of narrative or story in the mid-1980s as they found that this metaphor conveyed a precise and fruitful way to describe what they saw happening in their family sessions.

Acknowledging that a narrative never can encompass the full richness of our lives they quoted the anthropologist Edward Bruner: '…life experience is richer than discourse. Narrative structures organize and give meaning to experience, but there are always feelings and lived experience not fully encompassed by the dominant story' (White and Epston 1990, p.20). All human beings tend to organize and give meaning to their experiences in their life by turning their experiences into stories; and as they express selected aspects of their experiences in the performance of these stories the stories become constitutive – shaping lives and relationships. Again they quoted Edward Bruner: 'It is in the performance of an expression that we re-experience, re-live, re-create, re-tell, re-conduct, and re-fashion our culture. The performance does not release a pre-existing meaning that lies dormant in the text... Rather the performance itself is constitutive' (White and Epston 1990, p.20).

By the process of externalizing and thereby objectifying their private problem-stories the child experiences a feeling of distinction and alienation from these stories and he or she becomes free to explore alternative and preferred ideas about who he or she could be. This work of re-authoring in the therapeutic dialogues creates an awareness in the child of how moments where he or she defied the claims of the problem have already emerged and survived under the nose of the old problem-filled dominant story. And the course of therapy is seen as a 'rite of passage' from the dominant prob-lem-story to the alternative preferred story. By the decons-truction of the problem-story the child escapes the 'role of passenger' in his life and begins to shape his or her life actively by increasing the number of moments when he or she and not the problem is in command.

Encompassed in the wave of narratology is thus the idea that you constitute your life by the retelling of your experi-ences and by the performing of actions.

The constructivist's description of reality as subjective and the postmodernist statement that all knowledge is temporal invite the therapist to question his or her role as an expert. However, confronted with the child and the family in pain there seems to be a lack of an ethical dimension in the subjective postmodernist world. In view of this Michael White has argued that the therapist should attempt to make his or her relationship with the persons seeking therapy as equal as possible. This, as well as the position as co-author of the construction to a new and preferred alternative story, implies an ethical obligation, a responsibility and a solidarity.

And taking the same stance as Salvador Minuchin, David Epston has pointed out the importance of not losing sight of the objective reality because, although the constructivists claim it is non-existent, it is often a cruel, unsafe and unjust place for people to live in real life.

Case History: Kristoffer

Kristoffer, a nine-year-old boy, was referred from the paediatric department for persistant vomiting, which increasingly was a hindrance to his school attendance.

In the letter after the first session with him and his mother and father I wrote the following:

> Dear Kristoffer,
>
> It was nice meeting you and your mother and father.
>
> Obviously you are a bright boy who at the same time is strong, and yet now and then you let yourself be outwitted by the Sneaky Vomits who love to rule over you and to shorten your schoolday. But now you have put your foot down and are ready to fight the Sneaky Vomits.
>
> You and I created the following plan: you and your mother and father make a box on which you draw and paint in order to make the Sneaky Vomits curious. When they come near the box they will read: 'All power to the Vomits' with an arrow down to a hole in the box. They will assemble inside to enjoy their new great power over

you…but you will trick them by sealing the hole with tape and burning the box in the stove! I hope you will have them all burnt up but there might be a few survivors.

I will hear about that when we meet again in a fortnight.

Good fighting!

Your ally

Torben

The next time Kristoffer came with his father who, being an engineer, had helped him make the most impressive 3-dimensional graph.

Kristoffer showed me his diary:

Friday after we had been visiting Torben we made a box of the parcel in which the mobile phone had been and I drew upon it. I wrote 'All power to the Vomiters' and made a Vomit-man with a gold medal and his arms raised in order to lure them inside.

Saturday we got a letter from Torben. Reading it we understood that we had forgotten to draw an arrow down towards the hole. I did it and afterwards I painted the box. I made it yellow, green and blue.

In the evening we placed the box in my room and first thing on Sunday morning I sealed it with tape as agreed. Then we put it into the stove. It was on fire for three full hours. It was me who kept the fire going.

Saturday, Sunday and Monday I won the battles with the Vomiters every day. There were some acid attempts but I swallowed them so they did not become Vomiters and therefore I was in command all three days.

I made the registration-chart together with my father.

On Monday we continued the diary: As for the fight with the Vomiters the week has been very good. I have won every day. It was most difficult on Saturday and Sunday. Saturday they were just about to come up, but I think it was not ordinary Vomiters because my father also felt bad. Maybe it was the chicken in curry.

Today, Monday, everything has been fine. I am so glad that I am beating the Vomiters. Hurrah, hurrah!

...Today it is Friday morning. I will tell you more when we meet.

In the third session Kristoffer was in such a good fighting spirit that we ended up agreeing on a fourth and last session in order to celebrate his final victory and liberation.

Torben

PART 2

The Practice of Narrative Therapy

CHAPTER 4

Guidelines for the Initial Externalizing Dialogue

Dear Susan,

Let me give you a brief account of how the externalizing dialogue is carried out in the meeting with the referred child and his or her parents and siblings.

Michael White and David Epston have described how, from the first session, the problem of the child is consistently externalized as an unjust, tyrannizing, tricky phenomenon whom the child and his or her family are encouraged to look upon as an enemy which they can defeat.

The therapist should first engage in a warm and enthusiastic contact with the referred child or youngster and they should agree about a name for the externalized problem. For small children it is often a Troll, for slightly older children it may be a Monster and for the young adolescents the name which the family has given to the problem, e.g. Obsessional Thoughts, Temper Tantrum, Eating Refusal, etc. The spelling of the problem with first capital letter in the therapeutic letters supports the externalization and alienation.

The child is encouraged to describe in what way and how much the Problem has been able to sabotage his or her life, daily actions and relations. Having obtained a picture of this the therapist will focus on inviting the child to recall moments where the Problem had been just about to get the better of him or her but where he or she had been able to stay in command and defy the Problem. Having found and acknowledged one or more of these essential moments where the child has been in charge of his or her life and actions, frequently without realizing it before the therapeutic conversation, the child is confronted with the choice at the crossroad leading either to the continued role of a victim or to the role of a freedom-fighter.

Once the child has been engaged in the liberation-fight a diary to register his or her successes and temporary defeats is arranged for the interval until the following session. After each session the child receives a therapeutic letter which summarizes the most important information from the session and what has been agreed upon in a resourceful and supportive way.

In the following sessions it is very important to maintain the warm, creative and supportive relationship with the child and to secure confident assistance especially from the parents but at times also from the siblings.

Case History: Natasha

Nine-year-old Natasha was referred for paranoid ideas and depression. During recent months she had been having obsessional ideas about everything including the idea that minerals were living creatures with emotions and should not be thrown away as waste.

This had had a tyrannical effect on her family, which consisted of her father and mother, her twin brother Michel and her six-year-old brother Aleksander. The problem was externalized as an Uninvited Guest who had forced Natasha to think like she did, and a registration of moments when she herself was in charge was arranged in the first session. My letters to her illustrate the therapeutic process:

Dear Natasha,

It was a great experience to meet you, your father and mother, Michel and Aleksander because once again I learnt that families can manage in many ways when problems appear as Uninvited Guests!

The Uninvited Guest who came to your family some months ago has been very impertinent to believe that he has the right to decide which thoughts and feelings you should have and he has even enjoyed causing tears to come to your mother's eyes now and then. I can really understand why your father put his foot down a few days ago and said: 'Enough is enough!'

With good support from your father you have let your senses and intelligence regain their natural strength so that the Uninvited Guest no longer makes you believe that everything is alive.

You asked me how long I have been talking with children and I realized it is 29 years. In all these years I have seen that when children and youngsters decide to engage in a freedom-fight against their Problems, the Problems' knees start knocking and their teeth start chattering and soon they realize that they have lost their power.

Many children have benefited from making a drawing of their tormentors and hence sent them to another world either by burning the drawing or by burying them in the ground. You can choose what you will do.

We made a deal that you and your father would keep a registration so that I will be able to see the course of your freedom-fight when we meet in a fortnight.

You are already fighting well and I hope you will keep your good fighting spirit!

Torben

In the second session Natasha and her parents were present and the letter conveys the atmosphere:

Dear Natasha,

As I told you I am sending you another letter and I do so with great pleasure because I am so impressed by your achievements!

The Danish flags which are greyish on my photocopy fill me nonetheless with the same joy as the many red and white Danish flags you have given your mother and father in this way!

You told me that Michel gave you a little hug every morning and I mentioned he might do so to support you – anyway you deserve a lot of hugs because you have used your intelligence and strength in such a fine way. Your drawing of the Uninvited Guest is so fabulous that you could almost feel some compassion towards him, provided that he is not arrogant enough to believe that he can control your thoughts. One day he will vanish completely and all that is left of him will be the drawing of him as a memory of your victory.

I am looking forward to meeting you, your mother and father in six weeks.

Torben

Third and last letter to Natasha:

Dear Natasha,

It was an impressive diary which you brought this time! After having had to fight on some days at first, you have won a series of victories both great and small.

Your mother helped you write the diary so that we could read it aloud together and thereby remember how well you have dealt with your Uninvited Guest.

We agreed that it would be all right for you to count once in a while without calling it a problem. It's just like playing with numbers and as I told you yesterday evening I tried to walk along the subway to find out its length in meters. But unfortunately it was so long that I forgot why I was walking along counting!

We also talked about the possibility of burying the Uninvited Guest but we agreed that it would be wiser to put him into an envelope and hide him in a cupboard so you will know where he is and that it is you who is in command.

Finally we made a deal to wait two months to meet again and then have a party with cakes, juice and coffee to celebrate your strength, courage and victory!

Happy reunion!

Torben

Susan, everything was well when I met Natasha for the final session.

Torben

CHAPTER 5

Recruiting Allies

Dear Susan,

As I have already mentioned I always place great importance on recruiting parents and often also siblings as allies to the child in the fight to regain an active role in his or her life.

The child is asked how the parents and siblings should behave in order to aid his or her growing strength and autonomy in the struggle with the externalized Problem as much as possible.

Now and then other grown-ups such as members of the extended family, neighbours or schoolteachers are invited to acknowledge the progress made by the child. This is especially important in cases where the child needs to escape the role of trouble-maker, thief, disinterested in schoolwork, etc.

A few examples will illustrate the kind of letters schoolteachers may receive. The first letter is to the teacher of 11-year- old Bjorn, who was successfully fighting a Temper Tantrum, nocturnal enuresis and poor school attendance and concentration during lessons:

To Bjorn's Teachers,

We – Bjorn, his mother and I – have met today to discuss how Bjorn can best be supported in his decision to work on paying more attention during lessons so that he can benefit more from the teaching.

We have reached an agreement that you teachers should continue to act as you are doing, but that you should pay attention to signs of change in Bjorn's behaviour which indicate that he is taking part in the lesson more. If you do notice this it is important that you mention it to Bjorn after the lesson.

I will add that, using his new strength, Bjorn has defeated a Wee-Monster today, reducing its power over him from 80 per cent to 20 per cent! Thus there is good reason to be optimistic and to respect Bjorn's strength and fighting spirit.

Kind regards, and thank you in advance!

Bjorn and Torben Marner

The second letter is to the class teacher of the bright nine-year-old Henrik referred to in my second e-mail [see Chapter 2]:

Dear Birgit,

Henrik is about to overcome a Troll who has been preventing him from using the restroom. Henrik and I would like to ask you if you would look at his chart and remind him to fill it in. The reason for this is that the Troll doesn't like it if Henrik remembers all the times he teases him.

Henrik's fight has been very successful so far and therefore it is important to support him in keeping it up.

Thank you in advance!

Henrik and Torben Marner

Finally a letter to the class teacher of ten-year-old Lene in the middle of her 12-session treatment for school phobia:

> Dear Annette,
>
> Lene is successfully fighting her tyrant, Shyness, but needs allies. Would you mind watching out for occasions when Lene could have let herself be ruled by Shyness but fought herself free – and tell her that you have seen it!
>
> Thank you in advance!
>
> Lene and Torben Marner

However, Susan, not everything I touch turns out successfully. Once I made a handwritten letter to the class teacher of a young child during the session. Carelessly I used a piece of paper without the formal signature of the hospital.

A few days later I was phoned by an indignant school director. She informed me that a teacher had spoken to her because she didn't know where this strange handwritten letter had come from. Neither of them knew what to do until the director suggested that the teacher went back to the class and asked the child! I thanked her for the information and promised her, and myself, never to send an incorrect letter again.

Torben

CHAPTER 6

Registration of Victories and Defeats

Dear Susan,

As you know it is never easy to continue to improve one's behaviour or develop a talent without recognition from other persons, and here lies the obvious power of the registration of the efforts of children in therapy. In the second half of the first session the child will feel supported by his or her parents, siblings and the therapist enough to understand the distinction between himself or herself and the Problem. This externalization of the Problem has been called 'a linguistic dissection'.

Facing the choice of continuing to be a victim or fighting for freedom from the Problem, the child is invited to work for an increase in the number of times he or she defies the claims of the Problem. To keep a visual record of these essential achievements the therapist introduces the idea of a registration.

Most often the child grasps the idea at once, sometimes I show the child examples from other children with similar problems.

The registration is the witness to the power struggle between the child and the Problem. Once the child has the upper hand the registration is a source of enormous encouragement both to the child and to the family. Also it is a never-ending joy for the therapist when the child enters the office with yet another registration that shows an increase in the power of the child and the family.

Younger children often decorate their registration charts, older children make mathematical graphs and some fathers who are architects or computer specialists help their children to make artistic graphs.

The registration charts of victories and defeats are enthusiastically scrutinized by the therapist who focuses primarily on the signs showing a positive development and interviews the child about how this has been possible.

But the defeats should also be addressed by mentioning that they provide good training situations for the consolidation of the new power of the child. Sometimes the therapist may acknowledge that the Problem temporarily has the upper hand by a remark like: 'Bright children have bright Problems!' This frequently triggers a smile and more courage in the child.

Case History: Bjorn

Bjorn was an 11-year-old boy who had temper tantrums during which he would destroy his favourite toys. Also he would wet his bed at night and was unhappy in school. After the first of nine sessions I sent him the following letter which reflects our conversation:

Dear Bjorn,

I am glad to write to you because I think it was a very exciting conversation that you, your mother and I had last Friday.

I told you about Ole who, at 11 years old, had a series of problems much like yours to fight with. His life had been ruled by a Temper Tantrum Monster. Little by little we found out that in parts of your life – in your room, in your relationship with your mother and in your school – you too are being ruled by one or two small Monsters. Monsters love to live in messy places, and your mother said that in that case they should have a wonderful time in your room!

For a long time your Monsters have pretended to be your friends, but their true nature has come out more and more clearly. They enjoy watching the destruction of what you really love! It is impressive that you have sometimes been able to resist their temptation to destroy things. Such a counter-move scares them, while at the same time they are secretly planning new attacks.

Together we made a plan for the final defeat of the Monsters. You and your mother should make your room so tidy that the Monsters will do anything to find a messier room. Your mother should get hold of a cardboard box which you then turn into a Jupiter rocket. You will make a little hole on one side and write 'Messy Room' above it, with an arrow pointing to the hole. On the reverse side you should write 'Jupiter', but in mirror writing so the Monsters can't read where they are to be sent. Your mother will take the box to her work and make sure that it's sent off. She will know that the Monsters are gone when your toys and everything you really like are in good condition.

She will also see that you will have extra powers to fight the Wee-Monster who has had his own way for far too long. Now you can teach the Wee-Monster a lesson too. You can train your closing muscle by waiting a little before going to the restroom when you feel like going. In that way you can be even more certain that you are the strongest.

And you certainly have plenty of strength: I felt it in your strong handshake. I have great confidence that everything will go well and I am looking forward to seeing your daily registrations when we meet again.

Your friend and ally

Torben

The following letter was sent after the second session:

Dear Bjorn,

As we agreed, I am sending you a few words after our conversation.

First: a huge CONGRATULATIONS for sending off the rocket with the first and most wicked Monster!

Like you, I was pleased that the power of the Wee-Monster had declined from 80 to 20 per cent. That is really well done!

We agreed that you could defeat the Wee-Monster totally if you make a record of your victories as well as the victories of the Wee-Monster. As for the Anti-School-Monster, you told me his power is practically broken because it is several months since he was able to make you go home from school.

Keep up your fighting spirit and have a good Easter.

See you in two weeks!

Torben

After six sessions, Susan, Bjorn had regained full command over his life and with great pride and self-confidence he volunteered a couple of times to come back and tell visiting colleagues from abroad about his efforts and success.

Torben

CHAPTER 7

Celebration of Success and Advice to Other Children

Dear Susan,

I believe that many if not all therapists whose family interviews are based on externalization and other aspects of narrative therapy tend to become short-term therapists, because of the many surprisingly fast positive changes in the children. The therapist trusts that his or her role as an open-minded, caring and creative facilitator offers sufficient support to the child and the family for them to get back on the track of a normal development. When the child is finally victorious, and the Problem is either exiled, starved, burnt up, drowned or laughed out of the house, it is time for a celebration. Frequently this is a cheerful session with cakes, juice and coffee, a self-esteem consolidating interview about how the child thinks he or she succeeded and a chance to share important advice which can be given to other children with similar problems. At times the child is also awarded a Diploma after the final session.

Over the years Michael White and David Epston have both emphasized the importance of acknowledgement of the transition from a problematic child or youngster to a

person who is seen positively in the family, in the neigh-
bourhood, in the school and in other institutions.

In a workshop in March 99 Michael White demonstrated
how young, middle-aged and old persons all have a vital
need for such acknowledgement of their personality and
identity to be confirmed through the retelling of the stories
of their lives.

Case Histories: Line and Jesper

Line was 11 years old when she came to therapy heavily
burdened by obsessive thoughts. The letters are number 6
and number 8 from the eight sessions she has had so far:

Dear Line,

As I promised, I will just send you a few words about what
we talked about in our conversation. I noticed in your
registration chart that there is an ongoing battle between
your strong natural thoughts and the Silly Thoughts.

You agreed with your mother that you have been able
to keep the Silly Thoughts down in the last week, and that
both the contact with your classmates and your mood
have improved.

As a counter-move it seems as if the Silly Thoughts
have smuggled some ideas into your head that you have to
clean your things in your room unreasonably often. So
that your mother can support your natural thoughts I suggested that she could give you some domestic cleaning
tasks which would undoubtedly make your sound and
natural thoughts tell the Silly Thoughts to stop. The way
your own natural thoughts are fighting the Silly Thoughts
made me remember the little angel and the little devil who
sometimes are fighting in Walt Disney's Pluto, when he is
tempted to steal the bone from the bigger dog.

I explained to your mother that the Silly Thoughts would diminish and disappear little by little and your wish for autonomy and the joy of being with your classmates and friends would increase. We also arranged that you could have a magic box in your room to catch the Silly Thoughts.

Finally we made a deal that you would continue your diary and now and then write about some good experiences you have had with your classmates until we meet next time.

Kind regards

Torben

Two months later after the eighth session, in which a Norwegian colleague, Stine, took part, Line received the following letter:

Dear Line,

Like I mentioned when we said goodbye, Stine and I are pleased to send you this letter because we share the joy which radiates from you and also from your mother. It is because the Silly Thoughts have become pale and have been placed so much in the background that you now have a totally natural life as a 12-year-old girl who can discuss the tidying of a room, can manage school- and homework and stay overnight when visiting friends. You chose to start talking with me (and Stine) alone without the presence of your mother and afterwards you explained to your mother that it was because your problems are now not too great for you to manage on your own.

Finally you gave some good pieces of advice to other children, some which Stine could bring to Norway.

1. If Silly Thoughts or similar problems insist on being in command it's a good idea to have a magic box underneath the bed.

2. Another good thing is to have siblings and a father and a mother to talk with when you need support in the fight against your problems.

Your mother told us that she clearly experienced a feeling of relief in the family and because of it the family members were able to behave more naturally to each other.

All in all we felt that we could have a longer interval before to the next and maybe the last meeting. If everything continues to be as good as it is now we made a deal that you should bring a cake and I should provide juice and coffee to celebrate with you!

Moreover, your mother told us that you had said that it would be nice to have a photo of me on the wall and when your mother showed me that she had brought her camera I couldn't help but willingly join in with the idea.

Stine and I wish you good luck with your birthday party together with all your classmates!

Kind regards

Torben and Stine

Jesper was seven-and-a-half years old when he victoriously regained normal restroom habits and he gave the following good advice to other children about how to catch monsters.

1. Write a threatening letter to the Monster and pin it up on the inner side of the restroom door.

2. Use your biggest cardboard box first and change it into a good Monster-trap. Maybe you could make a hotel out of it and tempt the Monster with free food. On the box you can draw what the Monster can have: sweets, juice and cake.

3. Be quick when you close the little hole.

4. Make your father or mother help you to trample the box so flat and little that the stove can contain it.

5. Shut the lid of the stove so the Monster only can pass through the chimney as smoke.

6. Have some smaller boxes ready, in case some Monsters should have escaped the first trap.

7. If any Monsters have hidden in the garden they can be caught in a hole when they push and turn over a stick which is holding a heavy stone above the hole or you can pull the stick from the other end of a long line hiding behind a bush.

Diplomas

If the efforts of the child have been extraordinarily great or fast it calls for a Diploma.

Nine-year-old Karen was tyrannized by Eating Refusal [as you will see in Chapter 9]. As you will understand, there was a good reason for giving her a Diploma.

𝔇iploma

*This Diploma is awarded to Karen who in a
strong and dignified
way totally has defeated
the Eating Refusal.*

The cunning enemy had forced the weight of Karen down to 19 kilos, but supported by her two-years-older sister, her father and her mother, Karen succeeded to wrestle herself out of the grip of the Eating Refusal in a remarkable short time.

Karen wishes to forget her fight and therefore she doesn't have to hang the Diploma on the wall. But every time she opens the drawer where the Diploma is placed it will remind her that she has a good right to be proud of herself.

Congratulations Karen!

Torben Marner

Eight-year-old Andreas had been assaulted by obsessive thoughts insisting on reducing the kinds of food he was allowed to eat.

Diploma

Diploma for Victory over the Tyranny of The Foolish Thoughts

This Diploma is awarded to Andreas because, supported by his father, mother and two older brothers, he has won a great victory over tyranny.

'Enough is enough!' Andreas said and began eating pasta, farmer bread, lasagne, meat balls and liverpie!

Every time Andreas looks at this Diploma he can rightfully feel proud, and other people who are looking at the Diploma will know how strong and wise Andreas is!

Hearty congratulations, Andreas.

Torben Marner

Over the preceding months seven-year-old Christoffer had been suffering from an increasing anxiety which had prevented him from attending school, had made him demand the constant presence of at least one of his parents, and finally had made him increasingly stubborn about what and how much he would eat.

𝔇iploma

Diploma for Making The Great Anxiety Surrender

This Diploma is awarded to Christoffer because he, together with his father and mother, has not only quickly and skilfully fought The Great Anxiety but also the helper: The Great Stubbornness.

In his dream Christoffer was eating a whole pizza and then Christoffer knew that the victory was his: the following day he was able to eat a delicious real pizza!

Every time Christoffer looks at his Diploma he can feel proud with good reason and other people who see the Diploma will learn about the strength and wisdom of Christoffer.

Congratulations, Christoffer!

Torben Marner

Nine-year-old Julie was referred for evening-pains in her right ear, which no paediatric examination could find any somatic cause for. In the second and last session she told me that her situation was now under her control!

𝔇𝔦𝔭𝔩𝔬𝔪𝔞

Diploma for Wrestling Yourself out of the Power of a Teasing-Monster

This Diploma is awarded to Julie for her success in no longer being tyrannized by a Teasing-Monster.

This Monster had been able to dominate the life of Julie for a long time by daily pains in her right ear at nine o'clock pm., but now Julie has put her foot down and taken charge. By actively opposing the Monster and being preoccupied with something else Julie has experienced being able to cope with the reduced pains in the ear!

Thus deprived of his power, the Teasing-Monster one day will give up totally and disappear into thin air.

Julie can have this Diploma on her wall or in her drawer – no matter where, she has every reason to be happy and proud of her efforts when she looks at the Diploma.

Other people who see it will admire Julie and may ask her for some good advice.

Congratulations, Julie!

From Torben

Witnessed by Norwegian colleagues:
Jan, Hege, Ellen and Olaug.

Today, Susan, I still make diplomas but only when the bravery of the child has been surprisingly big and effective.

Torben

PART 3

Letter-writing in Therapy

CHAPTER 8

The Making of Therapeutic Letters

Dear Susan,

Before I address the therapeutic letter as an essential part of the narrative practice, I would like to emphasize that, as I see it, there are certain preconditions for working with externalization and other narrative ideas:

- The child needs to be old enough (four years and above) for the therapist to be able to engage him or her in the 'linguistic dissection' of the problem.

- The child should not be suffering from severe brain injury with serious learning difficulties, severe autism, severe mental retardation or other irreversible conditions. Nor should there be recent severe trauma such as loss of parents or other close family members due to accident, illness or war.

- The child should not be in an abusive environment.

- The therapist must be able to engage the parents' understanding and cooperation in the therapeutic intervention.

As therapeutic letters play an important role in achieving positive results within a limited number of consultations, it is my continual wish and aim to write a letter to the referred child after each session in all cases where the problem seems reversible. If the problem appears multifaceted, I often have relatively good results dealing with an aspect of the child's many problems, for example enhancing self-control and self-esteem through the externalization of Temper Tantrum.

Normally I write both the letter and a very short summary of the session for my files during the 10 to 15 minutes after the session. You need to convey your confidence in the child and the fact that you are looking forward to meeting him or her again, in order to make the letter a source of encouragement and support. Drawing on the moments in the session when the child has stood up to the problem, you acknowledge the child's intentions and actions in the letter. After this I contemplate which message would be most enhancing and stimulating from the actual session.

The formulation should underline the externalization of the problem, should be resource-focused, and should be written in a language that you believe will be appealing to the imagination of the child. In addition, you emphasize what you have agreed on as a way of keeping a record of progress between the sessions. I don't attempt to solve everything in one stroke, rather I try to consolidate the recent progress of the child, encouraging him or her to go on.

My description of the present situation of the child may differ somewhat from the reality experienced by the child and the parents; but remember, it's a supportive narrative and not an objective truth which is offered in the therapeutic letter.

David Epston (1994) has described how 'a letter should be a moving experience and act as a doorway through which everyone can enter the family story and be touched by the bravery, the pain and even the humour of the narrative'.

Case History: Anders

Anders was thirteen-and-a-half years old when he was referred for obsessive-compulsive disorder which had appeared a few months earlier with a phobic anxiety towards dirt, saliva (when his mother talked to him) and AIDS, with excessive washing of his face and hands as a consequence of his fear.

The family arrived on 6 June, the anniversary of the invasion of the allied forces in France in the Second World War. It was a metaphor that seemed to contribute to the quick relief from Anders' dramatic and unpleasant condition. I saw the family four and ten days later and could see how rapidly the symptoms decreased, so Anders was a normal functioning pubertal boy in the last session just three months later.

Following the first session Anders received this letter:

Dear Anders,

You came to the family session on D-Day having problems with Tyrants who unjustly claimed that you should fear saliva and wash yourself in ceremonial ways. Luckily you have had a wise and good counsellor and ally in the general practitioner so that you now are just as motivated to defeat your Tyrants as the allied forces were in 1944.

I suggested that your mother subdued her voice a little the next couple of weeks to avoid feeding your Silly Thoughts. Hereby they will be much weaker allies to your Fear. We agreed on a registration chart both for this and for those times where you outwit an Urge to have a ceremonial wash!

Remember that Fear and Silly Thoughts always will try sneaky counter-attacks before they are totally defeated – something also the allied forces had to learn on their way to Berlin!

Keep your fighting spirit till we meet again!

Torben

With great pleasure and positive feedback, Susan, I still write postsessional letters to all the children whose problems I have externalized.

Torben

CHAPTER 9

Letters To, From and Between Children in Family Therapy

Dear Susan,

To summarize what I have written to you so far, I would say that the apparent ease and elegance of narrative therapy centres on speaking against the externalized problem and not about it; on empathy in ensuring the proper timing of the invitation to the child to become the privileged author of his or her alternative story; and on practice in improving the effectiveness of the interventions, including the establishment of registration charts and the formulation of resource-focused therapeutic letters.

The use of letters in therapy, although mainly to and from adult persons or to the whole family, has been well documented (Palazzoli *et al.* 1980; Penn and Frankfurther 1994; Rasmussen and Tomm 1992; Shilts and Ray 1991; Wojcik and Iverson 1989; Wood and Uhl 1988). However, as far as I know, Michael White and David Epston are the first to address the letter to the referred child in the context of narrative therapy.

The letters contain straightforward acknowledgements of the child, and of his family and their efforts, using encouraging metaphors and at times fairytale-like expressions and small stories.

Sometimes you may find that my letters pay little attention to the literary background of the age and the social context of the child. However, it is my experience that the child and the parents feel respected and intrigued by these letters also because the letters convey the emotionality and creative ideas which they recall from the sessions.

Now and then my letter-writing gets an instantaneous positive response, for example by a mother whispering on her way out of my office: 'Peter was so glad to get the letter from you – would you do it again?' Sometimes a child has told me that he keeps the letters in an album. This emphasizes the fact that words in letters do not fade away but may be read and re-read.

The following sequence of letters to, from and between two girls of nine and thirteen years of age provide, I believe, a good illustration.

Case Histories: Karen and Lisa

Karen and Lisa were referred at about the same time for anorexia nervosa. Karen, nine years of age, 131 cm and 19 kg, needed six sessions from January to June; whereas Lisa, thirteen years of age, 163 cm and 31 kg, needed 18 sessions from September to September the following year for a total recovery. After her third session I sent Karen the following letter:

Dear Karen,

As I promised you, I am sending you a few words, partly because I found it so nice to see you looking so much better and taking a greater part in the conversation, and partly because I would like to remind myself of what we agreed on.

We talked about when you would return to being the 'normal Karen', and I was optimistic and said when the beech trees got their leaves. Your mother was a little more cautious and said June, whilst your father protected himself from disappointment and said when the summer had gone.

You said that your mother came closest to the truth. Nevertheless we agreed if I was right I should buy the chocolate for our little liberation party.

I am looking forward to meeting you again.

Keep up your fighting spirit!

Many Anti-Anorectic greetings

Torben

Karen wrote back to me:

Dear Torben,

Thank you for your letters. I am fond of them and I keep them. I try to get the eating refusal out of my life, even though it is sometimes difficult. But I believe it won't be that long before I am the 'normal Karen'.

Happy Easter!

Kind regards

Karen

In the fourth session Karen asked me whether I knew other girls with the same problem. I told her that I would ask Lisa if she could write her a letter. Lisa responded eagerly:

Dear Karen,

I hear you have the same problem as I do and I would be glad to help you if I can! You have already taken the first step and that is to realize that you have a problem. It is important that you look on anorexia as a tricky enemy and not as a friend!

Some code words that have helped me are: Openness, Harmony, Honesty and Help. These four things are very important in my fight against the wicked Troll!

In the beginning I didn't want people to know I had anorexia even though everybody could see I had a problem. I was embarrassed – but not anymore! If you are embarrassed too I will ask you to stop feeling that way. Many girls get anorexia; it is a dangerous problem but luckily it can be cured if you really want it to be and are willing to fight. People you tell about your problem will definitely not think there is anything nasty about it. They are surely so worried that they will be happy to hear that you are getting help!

I know it's a tough fight: I fight it myself. It takes time, but don't give up, look on the bright side – I'm sure there is one! Everything will be all right, but it is up to you yourself and no one else, remember that! I would like to hear from you some day. Do write to me if you have more questions you think I could answer.

Best greetings.

Your friend

Lisa

Karen answered Lisa:

Dear Lisa,

Thank you for your letter. I was glad to get it. I am nine years old and I am in third grade. I also fight to be the person I was before and I think things are better than they were some time ago. I look at photos of myself from last year to see how the normal Karen looks. It helps me to talk with my 12-year-old sister and my mother. I, too, think that harmony is important.

Yours sincerely

Karen

P.S. How do you become happy when you are sad? Do you think that you will be fat if you eat? I have believed that. Remember: 'Nothing is impossible for the one who has the will in the heart.'

Lisa answered Karen's letter:

Dear Karen,

Thank you for your letter. I just want to answer your questions.

1. I become happy by thinking of the good things I have. By thinking that there are so many who care about me. By thinking that this is a problem I will get rid of. It is not impossible to be cured and when I am quite cured I will be even more happy in my life than I was before.

2. In the beginning I too believed I would be fat, but I have thrown away these thoughts. The two of us

should not think about that any more. The best thing for you is to fight on, that's what I do.

Yours sincerely

Lisa

Five weeks later Karen wrote a second letter to Lisa:

Dear Lisa,

I know it is difficult, but now I have managed it and I hope and believe that you too will do it. Have a good summer holiday.

Yours

Karen

P.S. Don't let anorexia rule over you.

At the same time I received a letter from Karen with her advice to other children with eating problems. What she said she needed was:

1. A good doctor

2. To talk with mother, father and Kirsten

3. To look at photos (old)

4. To exchange letters with Lisa

5. To be at a school camp with classmates

6. To receive letters from the doctor.

As I mentioned earlier, Susan, [Chapter 7] very often the last session, when the child and the family is relieved from the tyranny of the problem, is used to let the child be a consultant to other children by suggesting good ideas like the ones above.

Torben

CHAPTER 10

My Epstonian Letter

Dear Susan,

A few years ago a colleague from Oslo asked me to write a therapeutic letter in order to bring new ideas into the individual therapy of a 23-year-old woman referred to her for anorexia and bulimia. My letter is based upon my notes from two workshops conducted by David Epston in 1994 and serves as an illustration of the stance, ideas and metaphors in his work to help persons out of the grip of eating disorders. The letter did not change the story of the young woman overnight but provided a support to the therapeutic process.

(*Talk against, but not about the Problem.* David Epston)

Dear Kirsti,

David Epston is a friend and a colleague from New Zealand. He has helped a lot of young women to escape a year-long prison in the grip of Anorexia and Bulimia. In the same way as him I have recently supported a young girl, nine years of age with a weight of 19 kilo, and a girl, thirteen years of age with a weight of 31 kilo, to see through the disguise of Anorexia as a friend and unveil its deadly temptation. Hereby they have regained the strength to actively resist Anorexia and by starting to eat they will regain their normal weight – and a normal way of thinking and an appetite for life.

(*Anyone who is able to distinguish between Anorexia and Anti-Anorexia can win his or her life back.* David Epston)

Distinguishing between Anorexia and Anti-Anorexia can be done by remembering at first a few moments and then more and more moments where you have refused to obey the claims of Anorexia about no food or sparse intake of food, or the claim of Bulimia about excess food.

I will ask you to use a lot of time and energy to recall these moments for they are the proof that neither Anorexia nor Bulimia have been in 100 per cent command in these situations; in these moments you have been the strongest!

Don't lose faith if you are not immediately able to remember an important exception when you were in control – all the people I have helped have been able to think of at least one exception during the conversation – but it is possible that because we are only corresponding by this letter you may have to adapt to the idea of a future exception.

This means, when either Anorexia or Bulimia – confident in their command over you – demand that you don't eat decent food or eat in excess, that you at the moment where you feel the Urge, instead say to yourself: Now I will rebel, I just won't accept being a marionette puppet of the Tyrant, I refuse to do physical exercise and I will have a decent meal!

(*Fears increase in direct proportion to the time they are not confronted.* David Epston)

Not only Fear, but all Problems who try to convince you that it is their right to rule your life, will shake in their boots and get smaller when you actively challenge them.

You may imagine that it is impossible or an endless fight and you will be surprised how fast your strength increases when you, finding it increasingly easy, repeat your Anti-Anorectic actions.

You go from being 'a passive observer to your own life' to 'a personal agent in the shaping of your own life'. A new story begins to take form, a story in which you, and not Anorexia and Bulimia, are the privileged person in the 're-authoring' of your life and relationships.

(*Anti-Anorectic actions are a fight for freedom.* David Epston)

Accepting the unjust tyranny of Anorexia and Bulimia is to 'walk into a concentration camp without a trial, without a judge, without a defender'. With great skills Anorexia and Bulimia are able to indoctrinate 'truths' and ways to live; truths which, after the freedom-fight is won, you may wonder why you accepted.

My advice to you is therefore: don't try to understand 'why' in this phase of the freedom-fight, but be actively rebellious and persevering in your Anti-Anorectic and Anti-Bulimic actions – and keep carrying on! I promise you that if you do as I say you will begin to feel the sweetness of victory in a few weeks and thereby get extra powers to continue to regain your life so that it will be both meaningful and cheerful for you once again.

Torben Marner

A letter like this, Susan, will always have an impact, especially when you have prepared the ground for it during the session.

Torben

PART 4

Case Histories Told through Sequences of Letters

Dear Susan,

In order to emphasize the variety of letters that can be of use as a support to the externalizing dialogues with children in family therapy, I will include some sequences of letters and let the stories and letters speak for themselves.

Torben

Case Histories

Case History 1 – Aksel

Aksel was seven-and-a-half years old when he was referred for assessment for a possible neurological cause for his lack of social skills and tics. In the first session I mentioned that, to me, Aksel's empathy disturbance seemed to be caused by late maturation and I instructed his parents how to train their son in social interaction.

The few tics I saw seemed more like a stress reaction than a neurological disease. Aksel and his parents agreed that we should work to help Aksel increase his strength vis-à-vis a Temper Tantrum who had been in charge for too long. The father promised to use his skills as an architect to help Aksel to make a registration chart.

After the first of four sessions Aksel received the following letter:

Dear Aksel,

It was exciting and nice to talk with you because you are an open, good-hearted and intelligent boy who understands everything I talk about. I suggested that together we could fight against the Temper Tantrum who has taken it for granted for all too long that it is okay to sneak in on you, make an assault and make you do things you sometimes regret afterwards, and which in any case are troublesome and don't create a good atmosphere in your home.

We agreed to see the Temper Tantrum as an enemy and that you and your father should make a chart as a kind of a diary which would show how many times the Temper Tantrum has been close to getting the upper hand but where you have said 'No!' and thereby scared the Temper Tantrum away!

I can't wait to see your registration chart when we meet in 19 days!

Keep your fighting spirit!

Kind regards

Torben

Aksel got the following letter after the second session:

Dear Aksel,

I am as impressed as your father and mother by how many times you have managed to make a Temper Tantrum stop!

When you consider just how many Temper Tantrums have attempted to carry you with them and how many times you have been able to say no to a Temper Tantrum and fight it – I find it really impressive, Aksel!

We made a prediction about how you will manage in the coming six weeks. And you and I and your parents, we all agreed that you will be even stronger next time we meet.

I am going to America and I will take your Temper Tantrum registration chart to show people I meet there what a seven-year-old Danish boy can achieve! When I return and we meet again I will tell you whether the American children are as full of fighting spirit and strength as you!

All the best from

Torben

After the third session Aksel got his third letter:

Dear Aksel,

Your second Temper Tantrum barometer shows clearly that it is you who is in command and no longer the Temper Tantrums!

Your father and mother were the best at predicting how strong you would be! You and I preferred to be on the safe side believing that the Temper Tantrums still could get you into a scrape and that you could slide into a fury when you felt wronged!

But luckily your mother was able to tell me that your class-teacher, Dorthe, had remarked that you have grown so much stronger that you are no longer ruled by a Temper Tantrum when you feel wronged – you may be sad but then she can comfort you.

Your father and mother also said that you manage fine at home and that has led to joy and admiration for you.

Finally we decide to meet one more time to celebrate the fact that the Temper Tantrums can no longer rule over you when they want to but can serve you sometimes when you decide so!

You and your mother will select a cake and I will provide juice and coffee!

Lots of greetings

from Torben

Following the fourth and last session Aksel received his last letter:

Dear Aksel,

Thank you for the delicious cake you brought when we celebrated your defeat of the Temper Tantrums!

When we said goodbye you left a big piece of cake for me and I chose to share it with my colleagues. I showed them your Temper Tantrum barometers and they are very impressed by your victories and by how clearly it can be seen on the computer chart which you and your father made together.

All of us who are sharing the last piece of the chocolate cake today hope that you will go on being proud of being stronger than the Temper Tantrums – and that moreover you will be naturally happy and naturally angry when there are good and understandable reasons to be.

A thousand greetings and good luck!

Torben

Case History 2 – Martin

Martin had suffered from involuntary sounds and tics (Gilles de la Tourette's syndrome) for four years. He was being referred from the paediatric department at 12 years old because an antipsychotic medication had had only a relative effect on the sounds but hadn't reduced an unpleasant urge to kick himself in the behind with his left foot.

There were good reasons for me to externalize the 'Tourette' as a tyrant, and with his brightness and sensitivity Martin took part in the dialogue straightaway and soon found no need to continue his medication. We met five times during nine months – Martin with his father and mother – while a 23-year-old sister participated by phone during one of the sessions. Because of his extraordinary efforts and achievements I facilitated a correspondence with David Epston in New Zealand in order to give him as much support as possible. The expression 'mental karate' I learnt from David Epston.

After the first session Martin received the following letter:

Dear Martin,

It was exciting to talk with you and your mother because both of you are fighting against Tyrants who try to keep you in their grip while you are doing your best to free yourselves from them.

You, Martin, manage to keep the Tyrant at a distance by means of mental karate but you still haven't summoned enough of your strength to prevent your Tyrant (the Tourette) from sneaking an Urge into you, which means that it gets power over you again.

I told you about Ole who learnt to cheat his Tyrant and since you are as bright as him I know that you too will learn how to do it!

Your mother indicated that maybe she has been spoiling you and that has in some ways made you more mature than your age and in other ways more dependent. And your Tyrant, the Tourette, has utilized that for the last four years. But now you have put your foot down: you have increased your autonomy by learning to separate clothes for the wash, by learning to use the washing machine, etc.

And you have humour (maybe the best weapon against Tyrants!). When your mother said that she was sure that Martin, the two grown-up siblings and her husband all knew she loved them, you answered: No, I don't! For one moment your mother didn't know whether you meant it, but then you calmed her: It was said for fun!

Your mother told me that after she came to understand of why she chose to divorce her first husband she got more motivation and strength to reduce the power of her Tyrant, Perfectionism.

Finally we began to make a registration chart with the title 'All powers to Martin – down with the Tyrants' to support your fight to regain your powers, defeat the Tyrants and win back the freedom you had before your age of eight.

I have a few questions for you:

1. Do you think that your and your mother's Tyrants come from the same family, so that the efforts of your mother will also reduce the power of your Tyrant and that your efforts will reduce the powers of her Tyrant at the same time?

2. Could it be that the weapon of the Tyrant, the Urge, in reality is hollow and easier to defeat than you might think?

3. Would it be an advantage to write down the days when you outwit the Urge (and by that the Tyrant) so we can look at it together when we meet next time? And do you think it would be an advantage for your mother if she did the same?

I am looking forward to seeing you again.

Your ally

Torben

Some weeks later I got a letter from Martin:

Hi Torben,

I was glad to get the letter from you.

There have not been so many movements, but in the evening when I go to bed there have been some sounds.

When I was in a badminton training camp for a week I really did not do any Tourette and nobody asked me why I kick myself in my behind because I didn't do it.

My mother is writing the letter for me because I am far too tired, it's 11pm.

Greetings

Martin

A week later Martin and his parents came to the second session. His symptoms were almost gone and he didn't want to take his medication anymore. We made predictions about the time of the final victory and agreed on a celebration party of chocolate cake, juice and coffee. I told Martin about David Epston's different Monster Taming Associations, and in order to find out whether Martin would be ready for sending an application we made the following letter to his friends and relations:

Dear …

As I am interested in becoming a member of an Anti-Tourette Association in New Zealand, I would like you to pay attention to whether I kick myself in my behind.
    Tell me if you notice it!

Kind regards

Martin

Two months later Martin and his parents attended the third session. Since two colleagues from Moscow were visiting me that day, I had asked the mother to bring their beloved little dog Sophie to the conversation so my Russian colleagues could see with what tolerance all kinds of family members were included.

Martin was appointed a consultant to both Danish and Russian children and his advice was: Be strong and hope it will end well. He could still feel the Urge to kick himself but now his self-control was so good that he didn't do it when anybody could see it. During the session an application to David Epston was formulated:

Dear David,

We, that is Martin, 12 years of age, his father and mother (and Sophie, their dog) and Dr Tatiana Serebryakova and Dr Andrej Mukhin from Moscow are assembled here today to witness Martin, who has been in the grip of Gilles de la Tourette for four years, regaining control of himself! I have mentioned that you are the president of an Association in New Zealand which has many subgroups, maybe including an Anti-Tourette section.

Please regard this as an application for membership of Martin (probably the first European member?!) who has been in control of strange sounds and kicking himself for three months today. To support his application I should say that Martin decided to stop taking medication three months ago.

Please let Martin, his parents and me know whether he passes the membership test!

Martin, Gunnar, Karen, Tatiana, Andrej
and Torben

A month later David Epston sent his reply:

Dear Colleagues, Martin and Martin's Mother, Father and Sister,

I have just returned today from an overseas trip. That explains the delay in my replying to your most interesting letter. It is clear that you, Martin, are a strong candidate for the Diploma in Habit-Breaking. And I understand it isn't easy to break Gilles de la Tourette habits. So I am very impressed by your application. However, I need a little more background information before any final decision can be reached. But rest assured, your chances are very good indeed!

Martin: I am told you have been in the grip of Gilles de la Tourette for four years now. Firstly, can you tell me why you decided to free yourself of this? Secondly, can you help me understand how you did this?

Martin's Mother and Father: Has this changed your opinion of your son? If so, how? Had the Gilles de la Tourette problem tried to convince you that your son was a certain way? Have Martin's efforts to free himself been an inspiration to you? Do you think he has been an inspiration to himself? To his older sister?

Martin's Sister: Do you prefer your brother in the grip of Gilles de la Tourette? Or do you prefer him to be a free boy? Have you found more things to like about him now he is free?

Martin: If the problem of Gilles de la Tourette tried to make a comeback on you, what would you do to free yourself once again? Am I right in thinking that you did this all by yourself and that you didn't have any help from medication? Did you use mind-power by any chance? Or mental karate?

Martin: If you were granted the application, would you be willing to counsel other young boys and girls from around the world who have problems like you used to have. Also if you were interested, you could also give talks to your class or show this Diploma to anyone who thought you were still in the grip of Gilles de la Tourette.

Martin: In general, are you finding life better for you? Can you have more fun? Are you more friendly?

Martin: I am just wondering. By any chance, do you possess some 'special ability'? I am asking this because you must have something very special about you to free yourself of this problem in three months without medication. If so, would you mind letting us know here in New Zealand what that special ability might be.

I look forward to your reply.

Yours sincerely

David Epston

For the Educational Committee of The Anti-Habits League (NZ)

Some weeks later I assisted Martin and his father and mother in the reply:

Dear David,

Assembled today, 10 December, are Martin, his father and mother and me.

Firstly all of us thank you for your letter which showed your interest in Martin's fight against Gilles de la Tourette habits and your support of his application for membership of The Anti-Habits League!

During the session the responses to your letter were:

Martin: I decided to be free because I was fed up by being teased. Moreover the pills did not work anymore, so I kept forgetting to take them. It was just something I wanted to do and I cannot explain it better.

Martin's Father and Mother: Martin is a much stronger person than we believed before. Martin's new self-control has eliminated the daily irritation which used to be present in all of us.

Mother: It has been a great experience to see Martin use his will-power to regain so much self-control.

Father: Martin has become more extrovert and has begun to take up activities spontaneously.

Mother: During the last six months Martin has become more self-conscious.

Martin's Sister phoned: Of course I prefer Martin as a free boy, but I love him, whether he is free or not. I have noticed the disappearance of the kicking and shaking of his head and I am pleased that he is not teased anymore.

Martin: If it does come back I will do the same as before: use my will-power to say I am fed up with the habits.

I do not know if my defiance can be called mental karate.

Father: For my part I think that Martin's will-power is closely connected to mental karate.

Martin: I would like to counsel other boys and girls, but I do not know beforehand how to do it.

Father: You could use your own example that it is possible to regain self-control.

Martin: I would rather not give a talk in my class or show the Diploma to my other classmates – apart from my closest friends – I don't want to remind them of something which is no longer present. I feel fine – at least better than before, now nobody teases me any more.

Yes, I have much more fun now, and have become more friendly, open and I am doing more things, e.g. accepting a role in a comedy and going to a disco-theque.

Mother: Martin said that he thought he would come back after a quarter of an hour – indeed he returned hours later, 11.30pm., warm and happy from dancing. Moreover, he has spontaneously started to make Christmas gifts in the club for teenagers.

Martin: Maybe my habit was not so severe as other children's and that's why my will-power has been sufficient?

Father: Martin is too modest, he understates his achievements and he has in his way a 'special ability'.

Mother: This 'special ability' is a stubbornness which has made Martin incredibly strong.

David, we – Martin, his parents and I – hope that these comments will be sufficient for him to receive a Diploma from The Committee for The Anti-Habits League of NZ.

Martin, Martin's Father, Mother, Rie and Torben

P.S. *Martin:* I give my permission to Torben to use our exchange of letters in his book about David Epston and Michael White – provided I get a copy of the book for myself!

In January 1994 the following Diploma arrived:

The Education Committee of
The Anti-Habits League
(New Zealand)

has awarded

Martin

its Diploma in Habit-Breaking with Distinction. It is well known that Gilles de la Tourette habits are not easy to break. For Martin to do so, the League believes that he had to use his 'special ability' to regain control of his life from such habits. It was not enough for Martin just to get fed up with these habits; he had to use very powerful will-power. Although Martin is very modest about his abilities, both his mother and father testify to the existence of this 'special ability' which they call 'stubbornness'.

The League considers Martin's accomplishments to be so impressive and enduring that not only is Martin awarded the Diploma, he deserves a distinction. The League was also pleased to learn that you, Martin, are having more fun in your life, being more friendly, more open, and going out more to clubs and discotheques.

The League is particularly proud to have you as an honorary member for two reasons: first, you are the first person to break Gilles de la Tourette habits that we know of, and second, you are the first Danish person.

This Diploma entitles you to assist any young person, friend or otherwise, who seeks your counselling to break habits.

Signed by: David Epston

Educational Committee

The Anti-Habits League (NZ)

The following December I received a letter from Martin and his mother:

Hi Torben,

How are you? I am fine!

I am happy because you have helped me so much. It was a great help to talk with you.

I have been elected to the council of pupils and chosen as the secretary. Our chairmen are two girls and they take part in the school-board meetings.

I have just been to the swimming championship and was the first in the first heat.

I wish you a merry Christmas and a happy New Year.

> With love from
>
> Martin

P.S. Yes, we are a little late in writing, and the school consultation will take place for the first time tomorrow. However, since Martin's class teacher hasn't contacted us we believe that there has been nothing to complain about. Moreover, Martin has said that his teacher has been boasting in the staff room about how good he is in Danish. She told Martin about it and he didn't quite like it because he felt shy.

As you can see Martin is now a member of the council of pupils – chosen democratically – and he is the third member on the board of the school.

> Kind regards
>
> Karen

Martin received my reply as a Christmas greeting:

Dear Martin,

A thousand thanks for your letter. It's almost like an extra Diploma or a Christmas tale about you, that you are okay, that you are elected for the council of pupils and that you were the first in the first heat in the swimming competition!

It's fabulous and shows the future is full of promise.

A merry Christmas to you, your father and mother and a happy New Year to all of you!

Torben

Case History 3 – Ivalo

Although this is not a typical set of letters I would like to share them with you, Susan, because they are an example of the creative imagination I believe you always come into contact with to some extent when you attempt to enhance the 'healing potential' in the dialogues with children and in the therapeutic letters.

Ivalo, a girl of four-and-a-half years old, was referred because she would only talk with her father and mother and her two elder brothers, who were seven and ten years of age. Her father was from Copenhagen, her mother is Inuit from Greenland. In Inuit language Ivalo means string of tendon or necklace. For various reasons I only had two family sessions, but a year and a half later I received a letter from her parents about the life and progress of Ivalo.

After the first session Ivalo received the following letter. Her father read it aloud and since it was the first time in her life that she had received a letter personally she carried it close to her heart when she walked around in the house:

Dear Ivalo,

I will ask you to get either your father or mother to read this letter aloud when all five of you are listening.

I was glad to meet you and I enjoyed the way you could make my doll's house orderly in a short time.

There is no doubt that you are a wise and clever little girl who has learnt a lot of things in four and a half years. But in one thing you have let yourself be fooled: the Stubbornness which maybe used to be a friend to you by protecting you from unknown things and strangers has now grown so big that it has become unfriendly and an enemy who wants to rule over you.

How do I know that? Well, your father and mother told me that a Big Stubbornness rules over you and does everything to prevent you from talking with your grandmother and grandfather and with the grown-ups in the kindergarten – and such a thing a friend would never do.

A little stubbornness can be a good friend, for example, when you have to tidy your room; but a Big Stubbornness is a lousy friend because it wants to be in command and to stop you from having a fun time with people other than your siblings and parents.

The Big Stubbornness wants to be in command so much that it even won't tolerate you talking with grandfather and grandmother. But listen now, you can become stronger than the Big Stubbornness and become the one who is in command.

I suggest that you pretend that you don't want to be the strongest, but that you secretly train at the kindergarten by saying a few more words than you used to, for example 'good morning', 'thank you' and 'goodbye'. By only saying a little more than you used to the Big Stubbornness won't discover that you are training to be the strongest and the one in command.

Are you ready to train to become stronger than the Big Stubbornness? I will know more about that when we meet next time.

Kind regards

Torben

After the second session I sent her the following letter:

Dear Ivalo,

Today I will tell you something I didn't get to write in my first letter to you.

Once upon a time there was a girl who was four-and-a-half years of age who lived with her parents and two siblings in a house by the sea. The girl was joyful and would speak with her brothers and father and mother. But happy and talkative as she was at home, she was silent and closed up among strangers outside the house. And all the grown-ups thought: How will it all end if she doesn't say anything and therefore nobody will know what a nice and bright girl she really is?

One night the father dreamt that he saw a little girl standing on the rocks by the sea a little apart from the other children who were playing, laughing and talking. And the father saw that the girl was surrounded by small grey stones which made a circle around her.

Then the girl called on a grown-up who was with the children – and behold: three of the small grey stones changed into pearls! Kindly, the grown-up came closer and the girl said another word – and again three small grey stones were changed into pearls.

And it continued like that: the girl began to talk with the unknown grown-up and one by one all the small grey stones turned into pearls. Finally the little girl could bend down and take the pearls, which now were placed on a necklace of tendon and she hung it round her neck. Happy and talking, she now took part in playing with the other children and grown-ups.

When the father woke up he knew what he had to do and together with his little daughter he made a necklace of pearls he had bought. She added pearls one by one as she became more and more free to talk.

Dear Ivalo, I am sure that, just like in the fairytale, your father and mother will find pearls for a necklace and give you some of them each time you tell them what you have been saying to the grown-ups in the kindergarten. Luckily the Big Stubbornness likes pearls and since it is not very smart it won't find out that you are outwitting it by talking more and more and thereby becoming the one in command.

Maybe the Big Stubbornness one day will say to the little stubbornness: Ivalo doesn't allow me to rule any more, so now I am going my own way. And that day you, your two brothers, Iviq and Uiloq, and your father and mother can have a liberation party with sweet things you like to eat and drink.

It was nice to see you playing with the doll's house and talking with Iviq when we met and I am looking forward to seeing you again.

Torben

However, I never met Ivalo again, but a year and a half later I sent a letter asking how Ivalo and the family were doing and got the following reply from the parents:

Dear Torben Marner,

Well, it hasn't been easy to find a date for a meeting and little by little the time has passed.

Ivalo is now in a kindergarten school which she is very fond of. And best of all – she has begun to talk with all persons. Not that much, for our little daughter is shy by nature, but the stubbornness in relation to her 'talking to people' seems to be defeated.

Sometimes we have talked about our meetings with you, about your doll's house, etc. Ivalo has been totally aware of her situation, her stubbornness and the problem it was to us.

Her senses are well developed – she has learnt to listen and remember and that is a big help to her. She has kept her stubbornness but we don't see it as a problem, rather as a 'tool' she will be able to use throughout her life. She has her ideas and she can stand up for them. It may bring her some problems later on but she has a great strength and we believe that she will manage all of them.

Why everything has worked out so well for Ivalo we don't know, but we believe that her intelligence and understanding of the problem have been the direct cause of the improvement.

Thank you for your interest in our family and lots of greetings from Ivalo and Iviq.

Kind regards

Merete and Claus

Case History 4 – Per

To give you an example, Susan, of a very recent letter I will end my little book by telling you about 11-year-old Per who came in as an emergency having threatened suicide and having had an enormous temper tantrum at home during which he had destroyed his room, had torn down the wallpaper, thrown pictures around, had tried to turn over a bookcase and swallow a wristwatch and threatened to jump out of the window.

He came in my lunchbreak with his parents but without his two teenage siblings.

During this first session I found him cooperative and well behaved and I sent him the following letter:

Dear Per,

As I mentioned to you I am writing you a letter so that you and your father and mother can remember everything we made a deal about.

Firstly I want to say that I think you are a bright, open and joyful boy who is full of strength and possibilities.

Three years ago the Temper Tantrum succeeded in sneaking up on you in a moment when you were not conscious of it, and since then the Temper Tantrum has believed that it is his right to come and rule over you when he feels like it!

Actually he has done it so many times that he has made you think that it is something that you yourself initiate when you 'go berserk' – but in reality it has been the Temper Tantrum who has set you off. But now you have said: 'Stop! – Now I want to fight to win back my right to decide!'

Your father has been stronger than the Temper Tantrum all the time, so every time he has been at home the Temper Tantrum has sneaked off with his tail between his legs!

Both you and your mother have said that you are ready to throw the Temper Tantrum out of the door so we agreed that you and your mother should keep a diary in the following way:

1. You will obtain a blue cross each time the Temper Tantrum has been just about to make you 'go berserk', but you use your strength to defy his claims to do it.

2. Your mother will obtain a red cross when she is able 'to sit on her hands', that is not going and fetching you back from your room but waiting for you to come down to the drawing room again yourself. If she by an old habit comes to your room

she will write a red minus and indicate how many minutes she had been able to keep herself back.

3. We also agreed that your mother on odd days should react as usual, that is breaking in when you and your elder brother are fighting, and on even days she should write down when she manages to 'shut her ears' and not interfere.

4. Your father should make a mark in the diary when he has noticed how you manage the tasks of your freedom-fight.

See you again in three weeks!

Torben

Per, his 15-year-old brother Christian and his parents came to the second session and Per received the following letter a few days later:

Dear Per,

As I told you during the conversation I am impressed that it hasn't been just another 19 days of normal family life, but that twice you have actively prevented the Temper Tantrum making you 'go berserk'.

We talked about the fact that your registration chart showed that five times during the 19 days you have been assaulted by some of the smaller brothers of the Temper Tantrum, but you declared that they too will have a tough time in future because you will do whatever you can to prevent them from getting command over you!

Both you and Christian have been very attentive to the moments on the odd days when your mother couldn't restrain herself from intervening in your brotherly teasing and fights and she has had to admit it three times to the chart!

But when you come to think of how many times she could have been doing that I would say she too has managed fine!

I arranged with your mother that until next time we meet she will draw a blue star for you and an orange star for Christian each time she notices that you have spent together nicely, for example playing with the model trains.

I look forward to meeting you again to see how many times you have defied the commands of the Temper Tantrum and earnt a blue cross and how many times the Temper Tantrum and some of his smaller siblings have succeeded in sneaking up to you and provoking a little rage.

Best regards to you, Christian and your father and mother.

Torben

Four weeks later Per, Christian, the parents and the 18-year-old sister, Tina, came to the third session, after which Per received the following letter:

Dear Per,

It was a lively and exciting conversation in which you all took part! The registration chart showed that you are a brave family. You have dared to spend a week together in a little Norwegian cottage even though that it is well known that close spaces easily create an atmosphere of tension.

But from the chart I learnt that you and Christian have had a series of cosy hours together although the Temper Tantrum seems to have been present and tried daily to prick you with a fork! We had a good discussion about how you could starve the Temper Tantrum and finally make it run away from the family.

Tina described how she was once helped to get stronger than her Temper Tantrum by a firm, goodhearted and a little oldfashioned school-teacher. It seems like being the youngest child in a family often leads to a prince-like situation in which you may feel it unjust to have to 'work for your living' when a prince normally has 'a servant on each finger'.

However, you pointed out that you will be 12 years old in three months, and at that time you will be ready to take on your share of the family activities and to modify your bad language when asked to do something in the house.

I am sure you will profit by becoming 12 and more mature, because that will improve your control of the Temper Tantrum and his siblings and that will make everybody respect you.

I am looking forward to hearing more news when we meet again!

Kind regards

Torben

Dear Susan,

Per's story in the family sessions continues but will, like every story, come to end one day. So will this story, Susan, and to conclude my account of letters to children in family therapy I feel like quoting the late Danish artist Hans Bendix, who once stated during an interview in his old age: 'I didn't achieve the level of the masters, but I believe I succeeded in becoming myself.'

Torben

References

Epston, D. (1994) 'Expanding the conversation'. *Family Networker*, November–December.

Epston, D. and White, M. (1992) *Experience, Contradiction, Narrative and Imagination: Selected Papers of David Epston and Michael White 1989–91*. Adelaide, Australia: Dulwich Centre Publications.

Haley, J. (1963) *Strategies of Psychotherapy*. New York: Grune and Stratton.

Minuchin, S. (1978) *Families and Family Therapy*. Cambridge, MA: Harvard University Press.

Palazzoli, M.S., Boscolo, L., Cecchin, G. and Prata, G. (1980) 'Hypothesizing – Circularity – Neutrality: Three guidelines for the conductor of the session.' *Family Process 19*, 3–12.

Penn, P. and Frankfurther, M. (1994) 'Creating a participant text: Writing, multiple voices, narrative multiplicity.' *Family Process 33*, 217–231.

Rasmussen, P.T. and Tomm, K. (1992) 'Guided letter writing: A long brief therapy method whereby clients carry out their own treatment.' *Journal of Strategic and Systemic Therapies 11*, 1–18.

Shilts, L.G. and Ray, W.A. (1991) 'Therapeutic letters: Pacing with the system.' *Journal of Strategic and Systemic Therapies 8*, 92–99.

White, M. and Epston, D. (1990) *Narrative Means to Therapeutic Ends*. New York: Norton.

White, M. and Epston, D. (1997) *Retracing the Past: Selected Papers and Collected Papers Revisited*. Adelaide, Australia: Dulwich Centre Publications.

Wojcik, J. and Iverson, E. (1989) 'Therapeutic letters: The power of the printed word.' *Journal of Strategic and Systemic Therapies 8*, 77–81.

Wood, D. and Uhl, N. (1988) 'Postsessional letters: Reverberations in the family treatment system.' *Journal of Strategic and Systemic Therapies 7*, 35–52.